How remarkable, yet so ~~...~~ Roseveare, to leave one l~~...~~ as a testimony to God's p~~...~~ in her life. *Count it all ~~...~~ ... for Christ,* delight as well as struggle in serving him, and the wisdom of a tested and seasoned disciple. As always, Helen Roseveare's total commitment to Christ coupled with her biblical realism shine through to both challenge and encourage us. Readers saddened by the thought that there might be no more Helen Roseveare titles will be thrilled; and first-timers will find themselves wanting to read more.

Sinclair Ferguson
Associate Preacher, St Peter's Free Church, Dundee

Count it All Joy contains wisdom I have come to expect from Helen Roseveare. She is honest. She is hopeful. She is an encouragement to all believers who wrestle with counting it all joy, even in the trials that come our way. It's an even greater encouragement reading this book on the other side of her home-going to heaven, knowing that her struggle is over and she persevered to the end. Let her minister to you in her discouragements, in her victories, and in her perspective as a believer who has finished the race and glorified her Saviour all along the way.

Courtney Reissig
Author of *Glory in the Ordinary* and
The Accidental Feminist

In *Count It All Joy*, Helen Roseveare considers God's command in James 1:2 to 'count it all joy' when we face trials. At the end of her life, the reasons for many of her own trials have become clear and joy comes easily. But Roseveare prods herself and her reader to learn to be obedient in the midst of a trial by rejoicing in faith, even if we never understand why God has allowed us to suffer.

I am glad that Roseveare left us this brief final testament to God's goodness when providence appears to frown. To borrow from the writer of Hebrews: by her faith, she still speaks, even though she is dead.

Betsy Childs Howard
Editor at The Gospel Coalition

Count it all joy, my brothers,

when you meet trials of various kinds,

Count it All Joy.

for you know that the testing of your

faith produces steadfastness. And let

steadfastness have its full effect,

that you may be perfect and complete.

lacking in nothing.

James 1:2-4

Helen Roseveare

CHRISTIAN
FOCUS

10 Publishing
a division of of those.com

Copyright © Helen Roseveare 2017

paperback ISBN 978-1-78191-061-0
epub ISBN 978-1-5271-0129-6
mobi ISBN 978-1-5271-0130-2

Published in 2017
Reprinted in 2018
by
Christian Focus Publications, Ltd
Geanies House, Fearn,
Ross-shire, IV20 1TW, Scotland
www.christianfocus.com
with
10ofthose.com
Unit C, Tomlinson Road, Leyland,
Lancashire, PR25 2DY, England

Cover design by Daniel Van Straaten

Printed by Nørhaven, Denmark

CONTENTS

Prologue

Recently, in my daily readings in Scripture, I came to a verse in the letter of James that shook me. It was clearly a command from God, and I instinctively knew that I was not fully in obedience to it.

I remembered reading in Frances Ridley Havergal's little book *Royal Commandments* that she had once set herself to read through the Scriptures looking for any command that she was not aware of in order to obey it also. Her yearning was not to break any of God's requirements and that she should be wholly obedient to all His desires. 'Keep and seek for all the commandments of the Lord your God,' she wrote, quoting from 1 Chronicles 28:8. She continued, 'We have even a little shrinking from this. We are afraid of seeing something which might be peculiarly hard to keep ... it might be enough to try to keep what commandments we have seen without seeking for still more!' I had thought to myself at the time, phew! I find it hard enough to keep all the commands that I do know – without seeking any others!

But here was the commandment in James that shook me: 'Count it all joy ... when you meet trials of various kinds ...' (James 1:2). Had I really read it correctly? Wasn't that going a bit over the top? I had fairly recently sought to come to terms with Paul's statement in his letter to the Philippians: 'I have learned in whatever situation I am to be content ...' (Phil. 4:11). I had even testified to coming to terms with that standard of acceptance of the Lord's will in my recent book *Enough*. But to 'count it all joy'? No! And the verse in James specifically says that the 'all' includes tough moments – trials. To accept these as part of

8

the Lord's will, yes, that is fair enough, but to 'count it joy' – I wasn't there yet.

So I began to think that perhaps the word in the original language that is translated as 'joy' in ours had a different connotation? To us it usually speaks of happiness, at achievement or of acceptance. Yet it is the same word as is used of our Lord Jesus as He faces Gethsemane and Calvary: 'Jesus ... for the *joy* that was set before him endured the cross, despising the shame, and is seated at the right hand of the throne of God' (Heb. 12:2, my italics).

Chara, the Greek word meaning 'joy', is used twenty times in the Gospels – often relating to our Lord Jesus. We find the word in Luke 8:13, when Jesus is explaining the meaning of the Parable of the Sower: '... the ones on the rock are those who, when they hear the word, receive it with *joy*' (my italics). Again, when the woman who had lost a precious silver coin found it, she calls her neighbours together and says, 'Rejoice with me, for I have found the coin I had lost' (Luke 15:9). Jesus goes on to add, 'Just so, I tell you, there is *joy* before the angels of God over one sinner who repents' (Luke 15:10, my italics).

Did not the angels, who announced the birth of Jesus to the shepherds on the hillside, sing of this same *joy*? 'I bring you good news of great joy that will be for all the people. For unto you is born this day in the city of David a Saviour, who is Christ the Lord' (Luke 2:10–11). One last example for the moment is when Jesus was preparing His disciples for His departure: '... you have sorrow now, but I will see you again and your hearts will rejoice, and no one will take your *joy* from you' (John 16:22, my italics).

So, if that is what chara means – wholehearted *joy* – can I honestly say that I 'count it all joy', whatever comes, even trials and heartaches and difficulties?

We can add to all this that in the psalter we are constantly exhorted to 'make a joyful noise to the LORD' (see, for example, Ps. 98:4, 100:1). In the letter to the Hebrews, the Christian brothers and sisters are actually commended for having 'joyfully accepted the plundering of your property' (Heb. 10:34) – again, I ask, isn't that going a bit too far? When Paul was writing to encourage the Christians at Colossae to walk in a manner worthy of the Lord, 'fully pleasing to him', he prays for them that they will be strengthened, 'for all endurance and patience with *joy*, giving thanks to the Father ...' (Col. 1:10–12, my italics).

My mind realizes that there is a parallel set of verses, based on 'giving thanks' at all times. In Paul's letter to the Thessalonians, he actually puts rejoicing, praying and giving thanks together in one sentence – in all circumstances! – and assures us that this is the will of God in Christ Jesus for us (1 Thess. 5:16–18). Likewise, in his letter to the Philippians, Paul says, 'Rejoice in the Lord always; again I will say, rejoice' (Phil. 4:4) and 'do not be anxious about anything, but in everything by prayer and supplication with thanksgiving let your requests be made known to God' (Phil. 4:6). These are actually commandments – not mere sentiments.

I was therefore forced to think earnestly, how can these commands be? What am I missing out on?

I looked back on what God had given me to write my book *Enough*. I am wholly assured that His grace is sufficient to meet all our needs, in every situation, through every trial. I began to see this wonderful truth was

God's side of the bargain. It is His grace that is sufficient – there is enough for each one of us to receive all that we need. And so what does our response have to be?

I then remembered the night that I first heard the wonderful Gospel – that Jesus, God's only Son, had died for *me* on the cross, taking the punishment of all my failures, all my sinfulness, and paying the full price demanded by a Holy God, that I might be forgiven, restored and adopted into His family. I entered into His amazing and overwhelming love. That same evening I was given a Bible. Dr Graham Scroggie wrote a verse on the flyleaf for me: '... that I may know him [Christ] and the power of his resurrection, and may share his sufferings' (Phil. 3:10). He also said to me, 'Tonight you have started that verse, "that I may know him": my prayer for you is that you will come to know more and more of the power of His resurrection.' Then very quietly, looking straight at me, he went on, 'Perhaps one day the Lord will give you the privilege of sharing in His sufferings!'

I had been a Christian about half an hour, and I was being told that it would be a privilege to suffer with Him and for Him! And yet ... yes! That has become the foundation block of my Christian life. It has to be my response to His grace: the realization of privilege, no matter what.

Romans 8:28 exhorts us all, as Christians, '... we know that for those who love God all things work together for good, for those who are called according to his purpose.' I have known that verse for years: I have preached on it; I have exhorted others to accept its wonderful truth and believe it. Yet suddenly I was seeing it from another perspective. In other words, God was saying to me that as I trust Him and seek to live in Him and for Him, then I can assuredly know that nothing will be allowed to touch my life by accident or coincidence. God is in control, and in fulfilment of His will – on a larger canvas than I can see – everything big or little that comes into my life is part of His purpose. That is utterly amazing! He offers me the privilege of being part of His purpose, part of His plan, moment by moment. So I can think of everything that comes as a *privilege*! Whether it seems hurtful or joyful, whether I think I can see a point in it or not, *ALL is privilege*. The next step, if that is so, is that I can say – and truly mean – that in everything I *can* rejoice: counting it all joy, even in trials and tribulations.

I now look back over my seventy years of loving and serving the Lord Jesus. It is often so much easier to see in hindsight how each circumstance worked itself out to be a *privileged joy*. Yet I am sure, as we all grow in grace, we will come to accept and understand this tremendous truth day by day without having to resort to, or wait for, hindsight!

for the final exams to gain my degree in medicine approached, everyone at mission headquarters was praying for me. God had wonderfully provided the necessary money to apply to sit the exams, to travel up to Cambridge and for a week's accommodation there.

The first day of the exams came … I had received the timetable of the exams – written, oral and practical – for the next ten days. Upheld by much prayer, I arrived at the examination centre – with some 180 other students – and we started off! They were a very intense ten days, yet I felt fairly satisfied that I had been able to cope with each exam as it came. Then, on the last day, the list was read out of those who had passed all eight subjects – male students first, followed by the women, in alphabetical order. My name was last on the list … and I waited … in vain. My name was not read out. I had failed.

Later I was told that I had failed only one practical exam (in obstetrics) – but I would have to sit all eight again. My heart lurched … yet I immediately decided to go for it and sit parts one and two together in six months' time. I went back to headquarters for more study and prayer. Six months later, I went through a repeat performance – but now with all twenty subjects in one go! Exams were spread over two weeks, with two a day for ten days. It was certainly going to be hard going, but I set out (I think bravely!) to tackle the whole lot – again hugely supported by prayer from all my friends at the mission.

The last oral exam was hardly completed on the second Friday afternoon when we were all called to the central hall to hear the results. My brother-in-law was also there, waiting for his results – and we had both bought a small gift for each other, ready to offer congratulations on having become doctors! Again I endured the awful waiting ... and listening to the slow reading of all the names of successful candidates. Then again, for me, was the heartbreaking silence when my name was not read out. Again, I had failed.

John and I still exchanged gifts, and I asked him to ring my mother and tell her that I had failed – I just hadn't the heart to ring her myself. How could this be? I was only training to be a doctor in order to serve God overseas as a missionary ... and so many had prayed for me. I felt shattered.

Later I was told that, once again, I had failed only one exam (in pharmacology) but I would have to sit all twelve exams of part two again. So followed another six months of intensive study – cramming my head with facts and figures, and seeking to memorize pages and pages of notes and textbooks! Then I went up to Cambridge again for another resit – and by God's grace and goodness, this time I passed!

Looking back now, can I truthfully say that I counted it all joy? Most certainly not! I found it very hard to come to terms with the trial – although I was certainly overjoyed by the final outcome. I kept asking, why had I failed? Why had this happened when so many had prayed, and when my objective was clearly good and certainly appeared to be part of God's will for me – to serve Him wherever He sent me, in order to use my medical skills to point people to Jesus?

For now my preparations continued. I completed nine months of study in Belgium to learn French and sit their exam in order to gain a diploma in tropical medicine and hygiene; this gave me the right to practise medicine in the Belgian Congo, their colony in Central Africa. Then I had six months of training at my mission headquarters, in order to be accepted into the mission to serve in the said Belgian Congo. After that I sailed out and eventually reached our work in the 'Heart of Africa': a six-week journey! Years later, though, I had an experience that recalled all that I have just recounted about my own journey (and tribulation!) to become a doctor.

We had established a small hospital in a clearing at the edge of the great Ituri forest. With it came the need to train African students to be 'medical auxiliaries' – not doctors, yet more than nurses – able to do most of the tasks necessary for caring for patients. We therefore organized an eighteen-month course of teaching, with practically no guidance from any government authority but with their permission. At the end of the programme, the first eight young students were accepted to sit the official exams. One failed – and he was heartbroken.

Seeing him in my 'office', giving him his papers along with the exam results and sadly explaining to him that he would have to return to his own village without the coveted diploma, we spoke together in French – the language of the government and of officialdom. I then invited him to come up to my home. There, over a cup of coffee, and speaking to him in Swahili (our common language, in which I could be better understood by him and treat him as though I was his mother!), I told him how I had failed my medical finals all those years before.

'You failed?' he exclaimed in disbelief!

To my African friends, this was unbelievable – they had come to believe that I knew everything! But I assured him that it was the truth – I had failed my finals. *But*, I hastened to add, 'I went back and tried again!'

After a moment's silence, he looked up and asked, 'Can I try again?'

'Yes,' I answered, 'and we will help you all we can to pass this next time.'

It was amazing to see the change in his face. He shook my hand firmly, assured me, 'I won't let you down again' and went back to the other students, with a fresh determination.

I was quietly amazed.

'Dear Lord, thank you for showing me why you chose for me to fail my own finals years ago – that I might be able to help this lad today.'

But I know that wasn't the only reason! It had done me no end of good in my own walk with the Lord to have to come to terms with His will rather than my own. Certainly having to study all those subjects for an extra six months had indeed prepared me for some of the extraordinary difficulties that I was to face in Congo – working on my own with no-one to consult, with insufficient supplies and often without sufficient know-how as to how to do what needed to be done.

Yes, with hindsight, I could now 'count it all joy' – but should I not have had the humility and sensitivity to have trusted God at the time, and known that He knew why it was best to be the way that He planned it, rather than simply my way?

| 2 |

From Ibambi to Nebobongo

Having finally set out for the Belgian Congo, I had arrived at Ibambi one Tuesday evening in March 1953, to a tumultuous welcome, at the home of Jack and Jessie Scholes, the leaders of our mission. At that time it was called HAM – the Heart of Africa Mission – but was about to change its name to WEC – Worldwide Evangelisation Crusade, which later again became Worldwide Evangelisation for Christ. HAM was responsible for the preaching of the Gospel in a region in north-east Belgian Congo that was about the size of the whole of the UK. Ibambi was the village at its heart, where the Scholes led the ministry in a Bible school and the Cripps, working with a national team, ran a printing press. The village was in the outskirts of the great Ituri forest – and so was hot and humid all the year round.

Initially, I had a room in the home of the Scholes, and from there I was asked to build up a medical service for the half a million people we served. Shortly, I was given a small three-roomed building from where I could make a start. Tom-tom drums beat out the message: 'Our doctor has arrived!' Then people, mostly women carrying babies and accompanied by small children, began to arrive – in droves, day and night, with anything up to 200 each day. I experienced the noise, the heat, the smell – and a growing sense of my own inability to cope – but I started out on what at first appeared an impossible task!

Almost at once, it was obvious that I must train a team of willing helpers ... and then build – a women and children's ward first, and a smaller men's ward to follow. All manner of people came – be they patients, be they builders, be they students! The work grew at an extraordinary pace, until in eighteen months the first group of eight lads was ready to sit the government's exam to become medical auxiliaries. We were all excited – and rather proud of our new homemade uniforms!

So we set out, in our three-roomed 'hospital', to develop a general medical service for our half a million possible patients. My newly qualified assistants were keen enough to learn, but their knowledge was so limited that everything they did needed supervision! And I had to spend so much time looking up things in my few books that I had brought with me – all university textbooks, and none with an emphasis on tropical medicine! It was all very frustrating.

Then one day a lad came across from the Scholes' house to ask me to go over there to meet with a committee of missionaries. I arrived there, unprepared for what was to come, and probably full of pride at what we had so far achieved. I was met by Mrs Jessie Scholes, who told me the committee of leaders were busy. She invited me into her room to wait for them to be ready to call me in, and then told me briefly what they wanted to suggest to me.

'The medical work is growing so fast,' she explained, 'that we all fear that it will swamp everything else here at Ibambi. And so the committee want to send you some eleven miles up the road to base your medical work at Nebobongo.' This was a small clearing in the forest, where Edith Moules had started the leprosy work of WEC some years before. There was still a 'camp' for the sufferers of leprosy, a small orphanage for the children of these leprosy sufferers, two brick-built homes for the missionaries involved in the care of patients and children ... but nothing much else. The clearing was largely overgrown, and a feeling of discouragement was heavy in the air.

My heart heaved at Jessie's words. 'This is madness,' was my immediate reaction. I felt angry. No-one had asked me for my opinion. Who would build the needed facilities for a medical centre to flourish?

Jessie suggested that we pray together until the committee was free to see me.

'Pray?!' No way, I thought. In my anger, I just wanted to show them how unreasonable was their suggestion ... and yet I think I knew that if we paused and prayed about it, God would ask me to give in and accept their direction, and not to push my own point of view.

Jessie sensed my rebellious spirit. She quietly prayed – and practically ignored me. Slowly my heart quietened, and I kind of whispered to God, 'Please forgive me and help me to accept whatever the committee says.' But certainly there was no bit of me that could rejoice in this decision.

The committee called me in, explained their point of view and suggested that I plan to move – lock, stock and barrel – in about four weeks' time. They would help me to settle in at Nebobongo.

I said nothing. God had won the battle when Jessie prayed – and I just accepted the decision. Yet I did so not with joy and gladness, nor with meekness and submission, but only out of necessity. In four weeks' time I moved.

Then I had to come face to face with the task that needed to be done. Patients started flooding in, once the tom-toms had sent out the message: 'Our doctor is now installed at Nebobongo'. I needed a consulting room, pharmacy, laboratory, outpatient hall, wards – and that was only the beginning! There would have to be workmen to build such facilities, yet such workmen, mostly married, would have families and so all would need homes. We would need a school for the children. I would have to feed them all, care for them when any were sick, train nurses and clothe them. The problems loomed bigger and bigger – and why had the 'committee' not foreseen all this? How did they think I could manage all this alone? And who was going to pay for it all?

Years later, as I looked back on that move – and all that followed on during the next eleven years – I could see, yes, God was in charge, and it was for the best. But at the time? No, I could not see this! I accepted the committee's right to make the decision ... but I felt they were being insensitive. Why had they not asked me what I thought about this planned move? Why did they think that a single lady missionary (trained to be a doctor) could actually become architect and builder, teacher of all age groups and in all subjects, provider of food for an ever-increasing family, as well as preacher and pastor of the local church, and the developer of a medical ministry throughout the vast area for which WEC was apparently responsible?

However, grumbling apart, I set out to throw myself into each of those roles. I soon grasped an idea (if not actually a vision) of what we needed to do, stage by stage. I sought to train different groups for each task. We drew up a plan of campaign and set about actualizing it month by month. On the whole, I enjoyed the challenge – and determined not to grumble but to see it through to completion. And through it all, I enjoyed the friendship of some of the African women, who loved me and stood by me – even when I made mistakes!

Agoya, a Bible school graduate, came to us to 'pastor' the church. He and I worked together so that Bible teaching became the foundation of every day, and prayer was the focal point that underpinned every decision. Agoya's wife, Mama Taadi, became one of my closest friends. We met together almost every day, for prayer and Bible study, and to encourage each other in our love for the Saviour. Another dear friend was Mama Damari, whom we trained as a midwife and put in charge of caring for the pupil midwives – and also for the tiniest of the babies in our orphanage!

But the weariness and load of responsibilities began to take their toll. Still I nursed the aggravating question, 'why?' – why did no-one feel they should come to help me? 'They' did not even seem to appreciate what we were doing! Buildings were going up; children were being taught in primary school; students were learning basic medical skills towards the coveted government's diploma to become a medical auxiliary; the teaching of the Bible had priority for the first hour of every day; outreach was taking place into surrounding villages to preach the Gospel, and give simple hygiene lessons ... the list could go on.

But I failed to see that, through it all, God was seeking to change *me* – to make me more Christ-like; more patient, caring and trusting; and always more dependent on Him for all that we needed. God saw that the best way to accomplish the change *in me* was at

Nebobongo, with all my Congolese helpers, and not actually at Ibambi, where I would have depended more on my missionary colleagues.

With hindsight in later years, I can see now what God was doing, and what He had planned all along to achieve – but why couldn't I have accepted that this must be true at the time? The fact that God was seeking to mould *me* into the pattern He had planned for me should have humbled me, and led me into an enormous sense of privilege that God cared so much for me that He would take the initiative to bring about the change needed. And such a sense of privilege at being God's child and in His care would indeed have filled me with the *joy* that I often lacked, and yet craved for.

years before. There were some tons of grass on the high-pitched roof, eighteen inches deep, but I had learned that we lose one inch of thatch every year due to the heavy tropical storms, so it was not surprising that the roof was beginning to leak. Whenever a storm threatened, I went round putting buckets and bowls to catch the worst of the leaks.

So when the dry season started, just before Christmas 1957, I decided it was time to take courage, to strip off the grass thatch and to replace it with permanent corrugated sheets. We had the expectation of at least five weeks without a drop of rain. As I wrote at the time, we stripped off the old grass roof. We then measured, marked and sawed the beams, carefully lowering them with makeshift pulleys into their new positions. When I went to bed, under the stars, gazing up at bare rafters and through to the dark arch of the sky, all was in readiness to put on the new roof the next day.

Suddenly, I was wakened – what had startled me? Searching round in the dark for my torch, I realized that I was wet. Then I heard a steady swishing sound. I cast the narrow beam of light around the four walls of my bedroom, through the cascading rain. The walls were being rapidly denuded of their lime whitewash; my 'pictures' (cut-outs from magazines in the main) were drooping and crumpled; and the floor was awash with lime and mud. My bed was soaking.

I crawled out, found a raincoat and threw it over the pillow and upper end of the bed, which was still partially dry from where I had been lying. I then collected an umbrella, crept back into bed – where I sat cross-legged, under the umbrella – and opened my Bible on my knees. I held the torch in my teeth and tried not to cry as I watched the steady destruction of all my possessions.

'... You joyfully accepted the plundering of your property' (or, as the AV puts it, you 'took joyfully the spoiling of your goods'). These words from Hebrews 10:34 almost mocked me as I sat there, listening to the steady patter of the rain and the rising moan of the wind in the trees outside. Vivid forks of lightning split the dark sky. This was the dry season, when it never rained! We had not moved pictures or mats or books because it *never rained* for the five to six weeks from Christmas to early February!

By morning, there was an inch of muddy water throughout the house, unable to escape because of the sills – carefully placed there to prevent water *entering* the house! I could not bear to look at the shelves of books. It was thirty-six hours before the sun returned. It was two days before helpers were able to finish sweeping water *out of* the house. Then the task of drying mats – and books – began.

The books had been carefully treated with shellac to protect them from going mouldy due to the humidity; now this so-called *protection* caused the pages to be sticky – just to add to the misery of being soaked! Each page had to be separately dabbed ... and the pages seemed endless. The work had to be relegated to the night hours, as ordinary daily duties had to take precedence. Self-pity began to rear its head.

'Do you love me more than these?' a voice asked me.

The question was not merely more than fellow-missionaries, nor merely more than African colleagues, but now was appearing to enquire, 'Do you love *me* more than your books?' I was being challenged to be real. Was my professed love for God a pretence?

If I really loved God as deeply and keenly as I said, how could I be so upset over the spoiling of a few books – mere books, mere material possessions? Had God allowed this situation to arise to make me face reality?

I had been called to take 'joyfully the spoiling of your goods' – a command even if taken out of immediate context. This was part of counting it all joy, in every trial and circumstance.

On this occasion, I knew God's challenge at once, right there in the midst of the circumstances, and I had to give an answer. This time it was not to be resolved only by hindsight. As I thought of myself, sitting curled up on the pillow, holding an umbrella up, listening to the non-stop dripping of the rain ... I could smile! But then, as I handled the sodden books, as I held in my hand a treasured volume given to me by my loving mother or a ream of soaking paper for typing up daily notes for class, a wave of tears blotted out common sense and the awfulness of the night's events struck me again. Eventually, I was forced to accept that what had happened *had* happened and no amount of crying would turn the clock back – and I thought I had put the situation behind me.

However, years later I faced an almost similar situation, and realized that I still had to come wholly to terms with God's providential love and concern for me, and not demand that things be different. When civil war broke out in Congo, we missionaries were captured by rebel soldiers. Thankfully, though after much suffering, we were rescued from captivity at the end of the year and returned home to the UK. But during the ensuing year, when the national army sought to win back the north-eastern province, my home was designated a 'safe house' for some 100 or more local people. They were bundled in and told to stay in, whilst the army sought out all the rebel soldiers in the area – and there was a slaughter. Meanwhile, at my home, those 100 terrified people – mostly women and children – had no toilet facilities and were forced into using the cement bath for all requirements, and they tore up my precious books to provide toilet paper!

I eventually returned to Nebobongo to take up the work again. My friends had cleaned and repaired my home ready to welcome me. But where were all the books? Where were all those same books that I had painstakingly dried, page by page, after the dry-season storm?! Then I was told what had happened to them.

Could I just accept the situation? Or did I have to go into another grieving reaction?

To take 'joyfully the spoiling of your goods' and to 'count it all joy' are God's commands. God enabled me to accept what had happened, realizing that the poor folk had really no choice. And what was the value of a book compared to the fact that God had spared so many of us, and was giving us the opportunity of continuing in service to Him?

| 4 |

Can you thank me?

After the committee had sent me to Nebobongo, for the next eleven years we built up the work there: caring for the sick; training students; opening a primary school; feeding and clothing the growing family. Then in August 1964 – as I referred to briefly in the last chapter – we were suddenly and abruptly plunged into civil war. We had no warning – I had not a radio at that time – but one Saturday, just after noon, whilst taking a short afternoon siesta, I was woken by the noise of the arrival of a truck and the shouting of soldiers. Heavy pounding at the front door sent a chill of fear into my heart. A bunch of wild-looking men, shouting at me in a language I could not understand, accosted me.

My senior helper, John Mangadima, appeared and translated what they were demanding. 'They have brought a wounded civilian', John explained, 'and they need you to see him.'

Civilian? Did that mean we were at war?

'I'll go over with you', John continued.

Together we walked across to the hospital and found the wounded man lying on a mat on the veranda. He had been shot in the chest, but it proved to be a very minor wound. After a clean bandage and a cup of coffee, the 'crowd' were prepared to leave.

I went home, but my mind was in a turmoil. What did this mean? What might come next? Who was fighting whom? To what extent were we going to become involved?

My diary of that evening (actually written as a letter to my dear mother, in an exercise book, as there was no way we could send any mail out) reads:

We played scrabble for an hour after they had all left ... and I slept well that night. At Jessie Scholes' request, I have two junior nurses sleeping in the house with me, though I'm not afraid of being alone ... We have taken one wheel off the car, and it and the spare, the battery and the coil distributor lead are all hidden in my house. I do not want them to take the car ...

That was the start of five months when a rebel army sought to take over the country and to topple the government of the day. We heard that two local chiefs had been brutally tied up and beaten because they had supported the government during the previous four years. For the first ten weeks, our captors allowed us to stay in our homes and continue with our work. They assured us they would not touch the white women: their fight was not with us but with their own corrupt government.

However, it was not easy: they watched everything we did and listened to everything we said. Rumours abounded on all sides. 'They' (the Simba leaders of the rebellion) forced us to buy 'party cards', assuring us that all would soon be peaceful and we had no need to fear.

The days then weeks that followed were filled with atrocities, frightening rumours and 'soldiers' coming and going. They were searching for three men they particularly wanted. They found one, and he died after horrible torture. Shops were empty; there was no money. Yet we sought to continue the work of the hospital. One night we performed an emergency caesarean operation, during which I endeavoured to teach John Mangadima how to cope with such medical procedures, if and when I was eventually taken from them. We continued teaching the Bible daily – until the rebels issued a new order: 'No more teaching of Christianity'.

On Tuesday, 8 September I wrote in my diary:

Sunday, a close encounter with the 'lions' at close quarters – God disabled them – Hallelujah! Ordered to strike us, they could not move, and were more afraid of our God in us, than we were of them. We then gave them coffee and the Gospel. Unnerves everyone, and leaves a sense of exhaustion. But our God triumphs!

Fast forward to Thursday, 29 October, and my diary reads:

They came, somewhere between 1 a.m. and 2.30 a.m.

I leapt up, pulled on a dressing gown and rushed to the front door. A terrifying voice screeched out to open at once to the Armée Populaire. I, together with the two young nurses, opened up the door to them. They swarmed in, using awful language, and searched the house, throwing down books from the shelves and crockery from the cupboards, apparently seeking 'something' I had hidden.

Then they left ... except for the head lieutenant. He called me back, into the house ... ordered me down the corridor ... and I knew I was encountering *evil*. I tried to run away ... they followed me ... dragged me up. They beat me and kicked me ... and drove me back into my home. As I stood, trembling, horrified, miserable, against a pillar on the veranda, the lieutenant stuck his pistol in my face, and demanded that I should declare that 'Patrice Lumumba is the Saviour of the world.' Others persuaded him not to shoot me (though I almost wished he would – my heart was at peace with Jesus). Driven down the corridor again, part of a verse of Scripture came into my heart: 'led like a lamb to the slaughter' (Isa. 53:7 NIV). I felt His strength taking possession in my weakness. He went to the shame of the cross in order to save me *and* He had not resisted that terrible night at Calvary.

Then it was as if He spoke to me: 'Can you thank me ...' and every ounce of my energy wanted to scream out, 'No!' How could I thank Him for this wickedness and evil? But His quiet voice went on: 'Can you thank me for trusting you ...' That was an amazing thought! For me to trust Him, yes, I knew that; but for Him to trust me was a fantastic turn of the situation. Was He saying to me, 'Yes, I could have kept you out of this situation: I could have rescued you ... but I thought I could trust you to go through this with me, as I have a plan and purpose for the future'? Again: 'Can you thank me for trusting you with this experience even if I never tell you why?' Somehow, in the darkness of that appalling night, I managed to say to my dear Lord, 'I don't understand what you may be doing, or who can be helped through this ordeal (I was certain we would all be killed), but, yes, if you ask this of me, thank you for trusting me with this experience, even if you never tell me why.'

Immediately I knew that He was with me, that He knew what was happening, and that He knew how this could help forward His plan in future days. Yes, the pain was still there – He did not take away the evil, the shame, the pain – but so too was an overwhelming sense of His peace, His presence, His love. I was bundled up on to their truck and driven off to Ibambi. The next day, when many others had been rounded up, a large number of us were driven off to Isiro, to be stood before a firing squad. The rebel soldiers understood that they had been ordered to round up all missionaries, but actually it was 'mercenaries' and they had misheard! So later, released, we were driven back to Ibambi.

We were only halfway through those terrifying months, but God was with us. And the question, 'Can you thank me for trusting you with this experience even if I never tell you why?' brought such peace to my heart. That peace brought a new degree of joy. Had I actually begun to learn the lesson He was trying to teach me to 'count it all joy' *at the time* and not only in hindsight?

Of course, there were many times in the ensuing months – and even years – when I could not rejoice, neither over the memory of those sufferings of the rebellion, nor during the problems that followed in the rebuilding process when we went back after the rebellion had been crushed. Yet now, with the gift of hindsight, I am amazed at His gracious hand of blessing, and how He has used me to comfort others who have gone through the misery and humiliation of rape in whatever circumstances – because I have known the *joy* of His presence through the same cruelty.

Still, I need to continue to learn how to count it all joy, even at the time of the difficulty, and not simply to wait until, with hindsight, I can see what God may be graciously saying and doing. If I really grasp that 'for those who love God all things work together for good' (Rom. 8:28), then I would know with quiet assurance that *nothing* can touch me, except He allows it. Everything that occurs in my life must have passed through the filter of His perfect will. So I can thank Him and count it all joy straight away, without waiting to see how it will work out!

| 5 |

Returning after the civil war

We were eventually rescued and flown home for medical treatment and time to recover from the physical and mental trauma we had suffered from five months of captivity. Then the decision had to be made about whether I could actually go back into the same situation, now knowing what lay ahead? Could I face it all again? The answer was a rather diffident 'yes'.

We went back early in 1966. Many folk thought we were extraordinarily heroic; others thought we were mad. It was neither of these. Although fearful, I just had to go back; Nebobongo was my home and I loved them all there. I knew there was work to be done, and that I had not yet completed what God had sent me to do, but I confess I was very fearful as to how it would actually work out.

The destruction during those two years of civil war had been enormous. Most of the buildings were damaged beyond repair. Our equipment had been either stolen or destroyed. The food gardens had been ravished and wrecked, and no-one seemed to have the energy to start planting them again – so hunger was everywhere. Finance was practically non-existent – there was no government oversight of the needs of the interior of that vast country.

Added to all this we were surrounded by 'refugees'. Countless thousands of Africans had lost literally everything. Then there were the endless queues of the sick and malnourished with every type of illness but no drugs with which to tackle the problem. Schools needed to be restarted and re-equipped with even the barest necessities. On every side was *need*. It was all very overwhelming – so much so that my first instinct might well have been to run. Yet my second instinct was 'no', I must stay to face the chaos and help to find a way out. But where could one start?

Into this situation came a government soldier from the local commander, asking to see me. The interview was brief and concise: 'We are moving south over the river to liberate the Wamba area from the rebel soldiers. Will you please come with us and set up a refugee programme to feed, clothe and treat the anticipated thousands of refugees that we know are hiding in the forest?'

'What help can you give me to handle such a mammoth task?' I asked.

'Nothing. It is over to you to get what you can.'

I left his office and walked out into the bright sunshine beneath the jacaranda trees. So what now? I felt so utterly inadequate, with nothing for such a programme. I needed help – in a big way! I made my way out to the airport, where there was a plane stationed, and hurried out onto the tarmac. 'Would they happen to be going to Kisangani [the regional capital], and if so could they take me with them?' I enquired. The answer appeared to be 'yes', so I climbed on board and we flew off. Terrified at the enormity of the task that I had got myself involved in, I tried to plan. What next?

When I arrived at the city, knowing no-one, I spoke to an army officer who had also been on the plane and explained my need. 'You need to talk to the President,' he commented.

He took me to their army headquarters and explained everything to his superior. The next thing I knew, the President wanted to speak to me over the radio! After seeking to outline the situation and the needs, he said (or at least we thought he said, but it was hard to hear through the crackling of a thunderstorm), 'Go ahead. We will send you a plane-load of drugs up from the capital Kinshasa.' The local authorities told me to be on stand-by.

The next day, I was told, 'Your plane is arriving!' and I was whisked out to the airport. A huge transport plane was taxiing in. According to my recollections, I hurried out onto the tarmac to check what the government had sent to me – nothing! It was an empty plane.

The pilot said he had been sent to collect all the supplies *I* had mustered and to fly them up to Isiro, and urged me, 'Hurry! I must be away from here within two hours.'

A frenzied rush around town followed. Entering each store, I asked for half their available stock of powdered milk, blankets and clothing, and so on 'to be gifted to our trip to Wamba to help the refugees' and they responded wonderfully! On the one-hour flight to Isiro, as I tried to get my breath back, I planned again what to do next! Who could I coerce to help me? What would we need to set up such a huge programme?

Two days later, we set off, with every moving vehicle I had been able to 'commandeer', all heavily laden, driving through heavy rain and miles of mud. And a fantastic week followed. Each day the numbers grew – from a trickle to a torrent! – until we had seen some 10,000 refugees. Nearly a thousand of the most ill were treated; all were fed; hundreds were clothed ... and still they queued! Meanwhile, the authorities assured me there were several other areas where they hoped I would repeat the exercise!

I was exhausted. In my book *He Gave Us a Valley*, the second part of my autobiography, I give the relevant chapter (chapter four) the heading 'How could I be so foolhardy?' This wasn't why I had returned to Congo; this wasn't the sort of job I had been trained for ... And then I was stopped in my reasoning. In that one week, I had had opportunity to talk to more people about Jesus and His love than in any previous week! Wasn't that what mission was all about? We are to 'count it all joy' – even the exhaustion; even the wondering if this was really why I had returned to Congo; and never mind if it appeared that this was not exactly what I had trained for! Truly God's ways are higher than ours!

On the long journey back to Nebobongo, with a small group of returning missionaries, I recall driving from the mountains of Rethy down to the foothills to Nyankunde, a small Christian village. Here we were to spend the night and here I was to meet up with Dr Becker of the Africa Inland Mission (AIM). He was a veteran American surgeon who had worked for over thirty years in the Belgian Congo and latterly in a small thirty-bed hospital in Nyankunde. When the civil war struck, he and his wife were exiled temporarily across the border in neighbouring Uganda, but the moment it was considered 'reasonably safe', they had returned and were already at work when we arrived.

Dr Becker outlined his vision of developing at Nyankunde a large inter-mission medical centre and a training school for national paramedical workers. The church at Nyankunde, he explained, was willing to offer us all as a medical team forty acres of land in the valley adjoining where a few small clinic buildings were already in existence. The immediate suggestion was to develop this land with a 250-bed hospital with a maternity complex, operating theatre, laboratory, out-patients building and eventually a new para-medical training college. I was invited to join the team and head up the training school!

We talked far into the night. The need was obvious; the means were non-existent! It would have to be team work. And would I fit in after years of running my own show?

The next morning my team and I left Nyankunde to drive over 300 miles to our village of Nebobongo. Eventually, and after an absence of over two years, on the Easter Sunday morning of 1966 we drove into Nebobongo to a tumultuous welcome from our African brothers and sisters, who poured out of church to greet us! Also awaiting us was the crisis of devastation, as described in the previous chapter.

A few weeks after arriving back at Nebobongo, I went to visit Dr Becker again – this time for a longer period. As we talked, we stirred each other with the plan for the future! If all five missionary agencies working in our province joined together and pooled our resources to create a new hospital, it would be adequately staffed and equipped to meet the needs of the province. After some ten days of prayer and discussion with Dr

Becker, we agreed in principle to the new vision – that it was the right way forward and we should 'go for it!'

Back at my own centre of Nebobongo, I met with the church elders and nursing staff to tell them of our deliberations at Nyankunde and the proposals of a new hospital and training college. At first they were stunned – I had only just got back to them; they had no other doctor; how could I ask them to agree to release me? For two days we prayed over this together as we sought God's mind. I asked them to trust me that I would seek to train African workers to come back to them and run our little hospital and dependent dispensaries – to a better and higher standard than we had ever managed before. Then we all went to meet the church council at Ibami where, after two further days of prayer, the church council and elders gave me their blessing, somewhat reluctantly, and agreed for me to move to Nyankunde.

Then I left to start work creating out of nothing the new training college of which I would be director, whilst Dr Becker would be responsible for the development and running of the hospital, as well as for oversight of the whole facility. For me to move from the role of doctor to teacher was what I had longed for throughout the previous twelve years!

Shortly after we had begun the daunting task of building homes for the students, the classroom block, the kitchen area and the dining hall, a new edict was pronounced from the central government in Kinshasa, which decreed that the directors of medical schools were required to be able to speak the three main languages used by officialdom, and to have completed ten years of practising medicine in a Congolese hospital. I could hardly believe my ears and I rejoiced greatly because uniquely I was qualified to fulfil all these requirements! God had known all along what legislation would be in place when this time arrived after independence in 1966. He had prepared me for this so that I could apply for government recognition for our new college, with myself as its director.

Counting it all joy then was easy, but why could I not have rejoiced during those previous twelve years as I fulfilled God's perfect will in me for the blessing of Congo with Nebobongo Hospital, without having to see how it would all fit together? What a wonderful Saviour we have! I am still learning to accept His will – and see it as good, acceptable and perfect. This is essential so as to rejoice in Him, even if, during the process of its fulfilment, I cannot really (or even necessarily) see the 'why?' in some of the more difficult times. And difficult times there were certainly to follow.

The group of us representing five different missionary societies were setting out to create a first-class hospital and maternity complex with essential auxiliary facilities plus a college to train young men and women to be nurses and medical auxiliaries. It was an ambitious programme by any standards and with practically no help from the government. In the college we had to 'invent' our own teaching programme; we had to seek our own 'financial backing'; we had to create adequate buildings with very limited guidance as to the standards required. But slowly the whole project began to emerge and come together.

New staff now gathering at Nyankunde from across the world were carrying full workloads. Dr Ruth Dix, our obstetrician on the team, working with AIM, was pouring herself out in the maternity unit, whilst her husband, Richard, was responsible for all the new buildings of the whole project. I laid my plans for the college – a classroom block, kitchen and dining room – before Richard and he graciously accepted to oversee the work. We planned to complete the basic buildings needed in under eight years.

I have just reread the 'diary' of those next seven years. Despite all the problems we encountered, God so graciously undertook the task for us and kept on reassuring us that we were indeed in the centre of His will and His purpose for the development of Nyankunde as a medical centre. There were moments when I feared there would not be enough money to pay the monthly salaries of all the workmen, or the weekly food for the students, or the petrol needed to run the college truck that was essential for transporting building materials as well as food and household goods. But, as the end of each month arrived, so did the needed finance! Truly that in itself is a story of miracles – it was always just on time, just the right amount.

It could have been a success story. The building programme, seven years on, was nearing completion and was ahead of schedule. Both male and female students were enrolling in increasing numbers and teaching was going well. Government inspectors had been and given us a very encouraging report, and the assurance that official recognition of the college as a training school for national paramedics was on its way – indeed was imminent! On the back of all this 'success', elaborate plans for celebration were being put in place by the staff for a few weeks ahead to show off all that had been achieved.

Then, without warning, rebellion broke out amongst the college students. For many months previously there had been a low-level undercurrent of discontent rumbling amongst them, periodically erupting into the open. And each time we felt we had dealt with the questions raised sensitively, truthfully and transparently. Now the whole college of around 100 students was on strike – they refused to attend lectures, to co-operate with the staff or to work in the hospital wards. They were angry, raising issues about their 'rights' to representation on the hospital board and especially the non-payment to them of government scholarships, the money for which they believed had already been given to the college but was being deliberately withheld and misappropriated by the staff including myself. Basically we were accused of having lied to 'feather our own nests' at their expense.

All this was despite the fact that each time discontentment had arisen previously, repeated reassurances had been given that the government had sent no funds and that student scholarships, although certainly promised, had not arrived and so there were no funds to distribute to them. Students had even been given access to the accounts to help convince them that we were telling the truth. This time, though, the students were not in any mood to listen to reason. They had called the strike convinced that they were being denied their rights because of intransigence and even corruption on the part of the college authorities.

I look back now, some forty years later, and yes, I can laugh at the situation. But at the time it was no laughing matter. For me, at least initially, it was a spiritual fight not to become hardened, or almost angry, at the unreasonableness of all the accusations. And what hurt even more than the students' total lack of gratitude for all that had been done for them was the apparent willingness of the staff to believe their accusations.

The small phrase 'what hurt?' became the stepping stone to bring me to my senses. God had taught me over the years that when I felt hurt, I was to beware! That hurt is 'I' raising its head and demanding its rights; it is not Jesus dwelling in me, in charge, in control.

The situation in college, and then in the wards of the hospital, was becoming very serious. I wrote a letter to Dr Becker resigning from my position as Principal of the college, thereby releasing the hospital authorities to move towards a resolution of the trouble, without my hindering them. I went up the hill to my home, lonely and sad beyond words, then flung myself on my bed in tears and asked God to speak to me. I sought solace in His Word. I was reading in the book of Jonah that day but my heart was closed and I could not hear God's still, small voice, seeking to reach into my heart. I read it again, and then a third time.

'Can you not see? I [God] sent the storm, and the whale, in order to speak to Jonah –

but all the other ships in the area that day were also hit by the storm.' God was seeking to speak to me – to make me more like Jesus – but others were becoming involved in the story because I was so slow to listen, or to respond.

'Am I not sufficient for you, but do you also want the praise of men?' I wept. 'Dear God, yes, you are indeed all sufficient. You have never failed me. Please forgive me – my pride in wanting to be recognized and thanked; to take home films of the college *I* had built, the students *I* had taught and helped, and cassette recordings of *my* choir; and to hear the praises of the team for completing *our* project ringing in my ears. It is not *my* work and *my* success, but the sheer privilege of being allowed by God to have some little part in *His* plan for these dear people.'

God won through; He graciously filled my heart again with His peace, and actually with the *joy* of being His, and the privilege of serving in His purpose. What an amazing God!

she died. Then, in 1976, I had to have surgery for breast cancer. Next came the question as to where could I go to recuperate? I had no home base any longer, other than the WEC headquarters. However, I still felt wholly committed to WEC, and its lifestyle, so the leadership therefore considered how I could best be 'used' within the family. They were reluctant for me to return to Congo in the immediate future, and so instead suggested that I considered an 'itinerant' ministry. At the start this was ill-defined as to what exactly I was expected to do and who was in charge of my timetable.

However, the proposed 'few years' stretched out to the next forty years! And these years were therefore lived out of a suitcase. I was very privileged as I travelled all over the English-speaking world, wherever I was invited. My task was to challenge anyone who would listen – churches, women's meetings, youth groups at schools and colleges – about the overwhelming need of thousands (even millions) to hear the Gospel. What should our response be to God's command to take His Gospel to every tribe and group, as in His love and grace He longed for all men to be saved? So how could we take that Gospel to all who had never yet heard it?

The challenge was especially to young folk, as they set out on their life, to consider 'the call to missionary work' as an option. Our focus was specifically those countries which, at that time, were called 'the third world': the developing nations, many of which were in Africa, that were often in great poverty and without the educational opportunities that we in the West so easily take for granted.

Basically I enjoyed the work – and I learned an enormous amount from thinking things through, sharing with others and being available to be questioned on almost any topic they chose: industry, safety, travelling, finance! But the enjoyment was tinged with frustration – so often I saw very little positive results, such as hearing that some had actually responded to God's call to go! After ministry in any one place, I always moved on to another spot. At times it was very lonely as there was no time to build up any meaningful relationships. In a sense, each day I had to forget yesterday and seek to build new relationships with another family for today's ministry!

However, I soon discovered that an important part of my ministry then, during all the travelling, was *to be available* to each family in turn – often in a home I had never visited before. Initially, each member of the family was kind and polite. Yet later, though sometimes not until just before I was due to leave, the mother usually began to 'unfold' and I sensed there was a need to unload – preferably to someone who didn't know them, and whom they might never meet again! Sometimes this did not occur until I wrote to thank them for their hospitality – then they would reply and possibly unload a burden. Over the years, many new friendships developed in this way – but this took time.

Yet I did eventually come to understand that this was actually a ministry that God Himself had organized *for me*; entrusted *to me*. As I look back, I can praise Him for the privilege of being thus entrusted – even if sometimes I found it quite irksome adding this responsibility to that of the actual ministry.

I could be scared at being considered a sort of 'know-all' – available to give advice on almost any subject. And yet I did not want to fail the Lord. It was probably a good thing that I was conscious of my own inadequacy, and therefore that I was forced to commit each confidence and questioning to the Lord and so to seek His enabling. This helped me to rejoice in Him more directly, knowing that He could answer each need, even when by myself I could not give a meaningful answer to some of the many problems with which I was faced.

Looking back over those years, I soon began to realize that there was more merit in taking several meetings in one place than always just one-off meetings. For example, at the Redruth Cornwall Convention I was asked to speak several times on the one title: 'Stir me!' They wanted to explore to do what? To go where? Who was to be stirred? Why? There were 500 youngsters there, and a real responsiveness in the air! In Northern Ireland the Glenada Conference offered the same opportunity. Then one summer I spent several weeks at the Kilcreggan Conference Centre, speaking each evening to all the holidaymakers, a different 200 each week!

I made several tours in the USA, with enormous opportunities to meet with hundreds of young Christians at the beginning of their lives and to challenge them with the fantastic privilege and thrill of being called into *His* majestic service by taking the Gospel to the unreached millions. We covered over two thousand miles and spoke to over thirty groups in just three weeks – and I began to sense the enormity of the task the Lord had now entrusted to me.

The invitation to take part in the Triennial Missionary Conference of all the student world in the USA at their Urbana Conference was a highlight in those first years of deputation. What an experience to look down from the speaker's platform and see row after row of eager students – around 20,000 of them! And you were given twenty minutes to challenge them! In fact, the first time I went there, I was asked to 'discourage' them! I was to tell them of the difficulties and heartaches of missionary work – in order to lead into the main challenge session. Then I was able to see literally *hundreds* of them stand to respond to the challenge of serving God full-time wherever He sent them. What an amazing privilege to be part of such a moment! *Joy!*

The following year, a tour was organized in Canada, and on into the USA again – and that tour included several Bible schools, with multiple chances to meet with students and staff. Then, after visiting the colleges of Minneapolis, Chicago, Bryan and Asbury, I arrived at BIOLA (Bible Institute of Los Angeles) and had a fantastic time with the girls! Initially, they did not want to welcome 'another missionary speaker', but slowly they thawed – and we became real friends. It was a privilege and *joy* to be with them.

In years to follow, I had a tour in Switzerland (using my French) and spent four weeks in Australia. I went back to Canada, with eighty meetings from the far west to the far east of the country, and the opportunity to challenge nearly 20,000 young Christians to move out of their comfort zone and give all they had to serving in a missionary situation somewhere in the world. I returned again to the USA, including visiting Moody Bible Institute and Wheaton College, where I witnessed such attentive listening and meaningful questioning. Then there was a tour of meetings in Finland – amidst the beauty of lakes and palm trees!

Every country had its own emphasis, as well as problems and difficulties, but each opened their doors to me to bring the challenge of the millions still unreached with the Gospel. In the following years it has been both exciting and humbling to receive letters from missionaries from every corner of the globe thanking me for some word at some meeting, which (unknown to me) pushed them to respond to God's urge to move out into missionary service. Thank you, Lord.

Every now and again, there was an exciting moment when my heart was caused to sing with *joy* at the privilege of being at the right spot and the right moment for someone in specific need. One occasion was in Australia, after I had spoken at a crowded women's meeting and was making my way out of the tent towards the luncheon tent. A lady touched my arm and said, 'Have you a moment to speak to me?' I sat down beside her, and she opened her heart to me.

'Five months ago, my two-and-a-half-year-old son was drowned in our family swimming pool,' she started – and I felt choked up. I could just feel her pain. I put an arm round her, and she continued.

'My Christian friends told me to praise the Lord ...' I felt a rising anger in my heart. How could anyone speak like that to a young mother in the midst of her grief? I was sure that my loving heavenly Father would never have demanded praise from her in such circumstances!

'And when I could not,' she continued, 'they told me that I must have sin my heart.'

I cried out to God, asking Him to tell me what to say to this little mother. 'Not in the future, Lord, I need your help right now.' But all that came into my mind was a sudden clear picture of the night I was taken captive by the guerrillas in Congo, nearly twenty years before. What was the connection?

As I have already recounted, I had been forced at gunpoint along the corridor of my home, in the midst of wickedness and knowing that evil lay ahead, when the Lord said to me, 'Can you thank Me ... ?' Yet all He was actually asking me was, 'Can you thank Me for trusting you with this experience [that is, with all this wickedness] even if I never tell you why?' I shared a little bit of this with the lady and asked her if she could thank God for trusting her with this tragic event 'even if He never tells you why'?

God cannot deliberately inflict evil on us: He has promised to give us all good and needful things out of His glorious riches in Christ Jesus. But if He, Almighty God, believes we are ready to be entrusted with a deeper level of sharing in the fellowship of His sufferings – trusting Him utterly when everything seems to cry out against such a trust – we must ask, 'Can you thank Him for trusting you with this awful pain and to guide you through this?'

The young mother reached through the darkness of her grief and she prayed through her streaming tears: 'OK, God. I don't understand You. I don't see where there can be blessing in this. But I want to thank you for trusting me with this tragedy.'

During the latter years of this itinerant ministry around the world, I was given the opportunity of travelling to some countries in Asia where I had never been before. Twice, I received invitations to visit Hong Kong, where the WEC Sending Base for Asia was located. Each time, I had the privilege of speaking to hundreds of predominantly young people in their teens and twenties. They were willing to consider the challenge of giving their lives to reach the millions of people in Asia who had never had the chance to hear the Gospel message even once.

Then, in 2003, came the ultimate invitation – to go to Afghanistan! Shortly after the defeat of the Taliban, I was asked to attend a small intermission conference, primarily to encourage and minister to the Lord's servants who had just returned to work in that country. I went – how could one refuse such a request?! When I spoke with the team, I shared how God had challenged me to trust Him even if He never told me why. Just weeks later, three of this team were kidnapped and endured a short but painful captivity. They shared later that those words strengthened them and released them to trust God through their ordeal. My visit to them also proved to be a wonderfully unique learning experience for me. As well as this, I was given the privileged joy of meeting in private and having fellowship with an Afghan Christian brother who, of necessity, had to live as a 'secret disciple'.

Over the years, though, I felt the inevitable awareness of growing older – I was often very tired, and each day brought its own new set of problems. In the preparation of material for meetings I questioned, was it becoming very repetitive? Was it still relevant? Was I really still in touch with the Lord daily to know His mind? Or was I beginning to depend on my own ability? There was a sense in which I was becoming a 'popular' speaker – and I sensed danger! But who should I go to for advice and prayer support? Or was it perhaps time I stopped? Who would stop me 'going on' in my own strength when I had really passed my 'sell-by-date'?

There was no-one actually advising me to bring this itinerant ministry to a close – and invitations kept coming in! These included an exciting tour of meetings in the beauty of Finland and another packed two months in the USA. I was conscious that my weariness was beginning to increase and also an uncertainty as to whether I was truly being pleasing to God, or just keeping going because no-one told me to stop. A tour in France and Switzerland certainly put it to the test as to whether I could still minister in French! Yet the Lord in His graciousness undertook every step of the way and enabled me to fulfil the ministry to which I was committed.

I remember clearly an exciting tour that was arranged for me back in Canada, which included visiting four Bible schools, with over 700 young folk at every meeting and a very real responsiveness. Then letters came, sharing blessings received as the Lord spoke to and challenged individuals. My heart should have been full of *joy* and rejoicing in the privilege He was giving me – yet I was almost grumbling. I was ashamed at my reactions, but I could not force myself to 'count in all joy'.

We cut down on the number of meetings we would accept in any month. I sought the Lord's mind for His comfort, and for assurance that I really was still walking in the path He had planned. I tried to pray more carefully and specifically over the preparation of material for every meeting, and not to be content with merely repeating what the Lord had blessed at a previous meeting. But still I lacked His peace, and certainly I was not counting it all joy!

Then, one morning, I received in the mail a copy of the WECCER (an internal magazine to all members of our WEC family). There were several articles, seeking to remind each of us just what is our mission objective. One stated that 'the will of God is that He ... wants all people to be saved and to come to a knowledge of the Truth' and my heart thrilled – a reminder of our basic objective. Another article, on 'The instability of men and the immutability of His grace' by Ronaldo Lidorio,[1] stressed putting (and keeping) God's grace in the centre of our ministry. Then there were two final pages by Susan Sutton on 'Waiting on God – how do we do this?' My heart warmed to what she wrote and I felt a growing hunger once again for myself to 'wait on God'.

Susan quoted from Andrew Murray: 'If we see ourselves (meeting together for conference) with one purpose ... to wait on God alone, opening the heart for whatever God may have of new discoveries of His will, new openings in work or methods of work ...

1 This article quoted extensively from Patrick Johnstone's fantastic book *The Future of the Global Church* (Authentic Publishing, 2011).

what would our conference meetings be like?' She went on, 'The process of waiting on God is threaded with prayer.' This is done in quiet trust, in surrender, in seeking wisdom, and then with prayers of thanksgiving and of commitment, with a determination to put into practice and *do His will.* Then, in the middle of that paragraph, she asked this question: 'What needs to die in me in order for the will of God to come forth?' And I found myself asking, 'What needs to die *in me for me to become truly Christ-like?*'

If one could grasp again these basics to all our 'missionary activity', surely any feelings of inadequacy and/or loneliness might have no place left! Whatever my 'feelings', I can relax knowing that He *is* fulfilling His will, whether I happen to 'feel' inadequate or not!

| 8 |

His grace is sufficient

Once, when it was nearly Christmas, I had been invited to speak to a special group of women who were all members of the Christian Prison Fellowship. Pat, my friend, and I went to join them as they celebrated their Christmas lunch. All had either a husband, son or some other member of their immediate families in prison – some for horrific crimes, some for the second or third time. All the women were sad, and not really willing to talk to us. God had led me to prepare a simple flannelgraph presentation on the words: 'My grace is sufficient for you'. Yet now that I was there with them, I was not sure that it was the right word.

As we tried to make conversation with them over the nice lunch that had been prepared for us, I asked the Lord to reassure me if this was *His* word for these women that day. Sensing 'yes', that He had indeed led me to that particular verse, I launched out. And the Lord gave me great liberty to exalt Him. Then I replaced the words 'my grace' on my flannelgraph board with the name of Jesus: 'Jesus is sufficient for you'. Whatever your heartache or fear, Jesus is able to meet it and to give you the courage to face what lies ahead.

Even as I spoke, I saw how exactly it was the right word for that particular situation – how good is our God! I couldn't have chosen a better word to meet each dear woman at the point of her personal need – without asking any questions.

Afterwards, one after another woman wanted to talk, sharing her own heartache, and asked me to pray with her. So for an hour we sat with them, sharing over and over again that His grace is always sufficient to meet every need, and to bring His quiet assurance and peace – even in the midst of turmoil. There were a lot of tears ... but, essentially, a peace and the sense of the Lord God's presence. I left these ladies feeling humbled; I had been privileged to be part of the outworking of God's purpose on that occasion.

About the same time, when I was already beginning to feel 'older' (coping, amongst other things, with increasing deafness and an awareness of the start of forgetfulness), a new set of pains attacked me. I had a few months suffering severe pains in my joints and muscles that were not relieved at all by the usual painkillers. Eventually, I sought advice from a hospital consultant, who made a diagnosis of polymyalgia rheumatica. I was given two options. First, to do nothing and accept the situation, knowing that the pains should wear out after three or four years. Second, to treat this condition with powerful steroid drugs and accept the side effects. I was weary with all the pain so the choice was easy to make: to go for the treatment as fast as possible!

'All right,' the consultant said. 'I'll recommend a prescription to your doctor. You can collect the medicine after a couple of days and you should be feeling much better the day after that.'

A quick calculation indicated that would take us to Friday at the earliest and Pat pleaded, 'Please, that is too late!' I explained that I had a very important appointment on the Thursday: the presentation of the Maundy Money by Her Majesty the Queen in Armagh Cathedral! I really wanted to be well enough to go and be part of it as one of the recipients.

'OK,' replied the consultant. 'I'll start you off right now. Give this prescription to your chemist and by tomorrow, if we have made the right diagnosis, you will feel altogether better!' And it happened! It was like a miracle. For the first day for months, the pain had gone and I could move freely! I felt like a new creature. Yes, God was indeed good to me.

Immediately, as I thought over the previous months and realized how God had enabled me to fulfil all commitments (including one oversees) despite the pain, I had a profound sense of *joy*. God had entrusted me with the pain, enabled me not to complain and, in His own perfect timing, had sent the necessary relief. Suddenly, I was able to say a heartfelt 'God is *good*' – so good – without having to wait to see it all in hindsight. And

I realized that God had brought me through yet another stage of the journey. Isn't He wonderful? He underlined to me once again that His grace is indeed always sufficient – if only I trusted Him more!

Epilogue

Almost there!

For about a year, I have begun to think that I am 'nearly there'. I am at the end of my eighties. I am increasingly forgetful, and also deaf – which tends to cut me off from interacting with others. This makes it more and more difficult to 'count it all joy', but God knows I do want to obey His every command.

The last book I wrote, *Enough*, surely said it all: He has enough grace to meet all our needs; His love is sufficient to go round all of us. And I was sure that His grace was sufficient to constrain me to obey His every command – and that included to 'count it all joy', along with life's trials and difficulties. I believe it was Billy Graham who once said as he was growing older, 'When someone asks you how you are, don't start telling them of all the aches and pains – they almost certainly won't want to hear! Just say: God is *good*' I felt this was a good way to tackle the problem of counting it all joy and I accepted his advice. It certainly began to change my initial reaction to discomforting situations. But before long I sensed that it was becoming like a mantra. Almost automatically I would reply to folk with 'God is *good*'. Of course, it was true – God *is* good, always good, irrespective of my feelings. But was that really the same as a positive realization that in each and every circumstance I could 'count it all joy'?

Then I was asked to write a brief word of commendation to a new book from J. I. Packer: *Finishing Our Course with Joy*. I was challenged anew with a great longing to finish *my* 'course' with *joy*. How good is our God to give us such a challenge and to fill our hearts with a longing to actually *do* so, not just to talk about it! Yes, I believe I am almost there!

In my daily Bible readings in preparation for Easter 2014, my passage for study was the last three chapters in St Matthew's Gospel. My heart was deeply moved in Matthew 26. This chapter starts with hearing the religious leaders of the day planning how to trap and kill Jesus. The section ends with the shocking fact that one of His disciples was prepared to sell Jesus to these evil men. Between the two events there is the beautiful incident of an unnamed woman coming up to Jesus and breaking a flask of very precious ointment over His head as an act of anointing. She gave the *best* she had out of her love for Him, to honour Him as King and in preparation for His forthcoming burial – an honour the Roman authorities would never bestow on Him. It was without doubt an extravagant act. The disciples thought it a great waste of money, but Jesus saw it differently. Her love overflowed for Him, and He called her action 'a beautiful thing' (Matt. 26:10).

Then I turned to read the explanatory note on Matthew 26:1–16 written by Bishop Graham Cray in the devotional material I was using.[1] He pointed out that her anointing of Jesus was not 'despite His impending death: it is *for* His death'. Bishop Cray likened what Jesus was about to do for us, as He died on the cross, to the extravagant act of love this woman had just done for Him. My heart welled up. I wanted to cry out to the dear Lord, 'O, my Lord Jesus, that is what I want to do for you. Right to the end, may I give *all*, even the very best, to show my *love* to you, who gave your all for me. May I hold nothing back. And in giving all, surely I must "count it all joy" that you actually allow me – more, you invite me – to give my all.'

Thank you, dearest Lord.

---

1 Bishop Graham Cray, writing for Monday 7 April 2014 in *Encounter with God* (Scripture Union, 2014).

| Postscript |

A life of privilege by Louis Sutton

Helen Roseveare went to be with her Lord on 7 December 2016, at the age of ninety-one. At her memorial service, on 18 March 2017, Louis Sutton, the international director of WEC, gave the following address in appreciation of her life – a life in which she counted it as a privilege to serve and suffer for Jesus. This seems a fitting way to end the book.

Whatever happens, conduct yourselves in a manner worthy of the gospel of Christ. Then, whether I come and see you or only hear about you in my absence, I will know that you stand firm in one spirit, contending as one man for the faith of the gospel without being frightened in any way by those who oppose you. This is a sign to them that they will be destroyed, but that you will be saved – and that by God. For it has been granted to you on behalf of Christ not only to believe in him, but also to suffer for him, since you are going through the same struggle you saw I had, and now hear that I still have.

(Phil. 1: 27–29, NIV)

Helen's one word

Helen Roseveare, throughout her life, spoke on many themes, told many stories and used many works repeatedly. But if you were to name one word that was central to her life, that was very precious to her, that she kept coming back to over and over, what word would that be? (Other, of course, than the word 'Jesus'.)

Dr Pat could no doubt give us the best answer. But I think she and many of us would say that one word that was central to Helen's life was the word 'privilege'.

Helen spoke of privilege with a glimmer of joy. As is clear from her writing in this book, the word privilege became very precious to her. She spoke throughout her life of the privilege of serving Jesus. She spoke of the privilege of being a missionary, of being a medical doctor. She spoke of the privilege of taking the Gospel of Jesus to those who have never heard the good news.

But she also spoke of privilege in deeper ways. She spoke of privilege in the midst of suffering and pain. She spoke of the privilege of sharing in the sufferings of Jesus.

One familiar story of Helen, recounted again in this book, is that, while in the Congo during the Simba rebellion, she was captured by rebel soldiers, brutally beaten, her teeth broken and raped. And in the midst of that painful experience, she spoke of the Lord meeting her in those moments. She said, 'In the midst of darkness and loneliness He, Jesus, met with me ... in His love He breathed a word into my troubled mind. The word was: "privilege." ... He didn't take away the pain, or cruelty, or humiliation. No! It was all there. But now it was altogether different. It was with Him, for Him, in Him.'

It was privilege. This is privilege in the deepest, most profound sense.

As we remember Helen Roseveare, I want us to look at what deep truth Helen had discovered that enabled her to embrace privilege like this ... in this deepest sense ... in this deepest biblical view of privilege.

The word 'privilege'

In general usage, we use the word 'privilege' in many different ways. We can use the word lightly. I could say it is a privilege for me to be here tonight [at Helen's memorial service]. I can say it is a privilege for me to be here in Northern Ireland for the first time. I could say it was a privilege to eat real fish and chips, and delicious cream potatoes, here in Northern Ireland! In those cases, we use the word 'privilege' as a synonym for 'a nice thing'.

Sometimes we use the word 'privilege' a little deeper. We use it in the sense of an honour, something that not everyone gets to do or experience. It was a privilege for those of you here tonight who knew Helen

Roseveare personally. It was a privilege for those of you who heard her speak in person.

Certainly it was a privilege for me and my wife, Susan, to hear Helen speak at the Urbana conference (a triennial missionary conference for students in America) in 1976. That changed our lives, and Helen's message was a part of that.

There was Helen, down on stage, standing in an auditorium before 17,000 university students. She used a visual aid, as she often did. It was one of her favourites. She had a huge, artificial tree on stage. And at each point in her message, as she spoke of the challenges of her life in the Congo, her hardships and failures, she would pluck off a leaf, or break off a branch, even stripping off the bark. At the end, all that was left was a solitary, polished shaft: the trunk of the tree.

Then, in a powerful moment, she read from Isaiah 49:2–3:

> He made me into a polished arrow and
> concealed me in his quiver.
> He said to me, 'You are my servant,
> Israel, in whom I will display my splendour.
>
> (NIV)

She spoke of the cost of declaring His glory. Then she said, 'Looking back, one has tried to count the cost, but I found it all swallowed up in privilege. The cost suddenly seemed very small and transient in the greatness and permanence of the privilege.'

To us, 17,000 students wide-eyed with tears, the cost didn't seem very small or very transient. But, somehow, something in the way Helen spoke didn't keep me and Susan away. When Billy Graham gave the closing invitation, this time not an invitation to salvation, but an invitation to commit our lives to missions, Susan and I stood up with thousands of other students, raised our hands and said, 'Yes. We will do anything, go anywhere, whatever you want, Lord, to be a part of your great love for the world.' It was a privilege to have been there at that moment when God was speaking through Helen.

Some years later, Susan and I were having tea with Helen at our WEC USA headquarters. I mentioned to Helen, 'It must be wonderful to have the gift of encouraging so many people into missions.' She replied with a glimmer in her eyes saying, 'I don't think I have the gift of encouraging people into missions. In fact, I think I have the gift of discouraging people from going into missions. Then if God calls them, they know they are really called.' For all of us who have heard Helen speaking, it has been a privilege, a gift, an honour that not everyone has been given.

'Privilege' defined

I believe 'gift' and 'honour' would be parts of a simple definition of privilege. Here's mine: privilege is the gift (or honour) of doing something valuable that not everyone gets to do.

It is not a privilege, in the strictest sense, to do something no-one wants to do anyway. Try telling your young people that doing their homework is a privilege! Nor is it a privilege, in the strictest sense, to do something everyone does anyway. It would not be appropriate for me to say that you have the privilege of coming to this church tonight in order to breathe. But privilege is the gift of doing (or experiencing) something of value that not everyone gets to experience.

I think Helen understood privilege like this. But she also understood it at a deeper, more profound level – as the deepest expression of biblical privilege. Helen understood this. The apostle Paul understood. The Macedonian churches in 2 Corinthians 8 understood it too.

Paul describes these Macedonians in this way: 'Out of the most severe trial, their overwhelming joy and their extreme poverty welled up in rich generosity ... they urgently pleaded with us for the privilege of sharing in this service.' (2 Cor. 8:2, 4, NIV).

Most of us, in a severe trial of extreme poverty, would not count giving to others as a privilege. Most of us, in the midst of being beaten and raped, could not embrace the word 'privilege'. But Helen did. Paul did. The Macedonians did.

How? What enabled them to count as privilege such hard things, and count it with joy?

Privilege, we said, was doing something of value. I think you would agree that the value of that 'something' can be increased if that 'something' is connected to or contributes to something greater. It is increased to the degree that it contributes to a greater goal.

Let me illustrate. Like Helen, I too was a medical missionary in Africa. Like her, we had to adapt to working with no electricity. There was a time in the country of Chad when I was performing an operation: a caesarean. It was taking place at night, dependent upon a generator for power. But then the generator failed, everyone was plunged into darkness and the outcome of the operation was in jeopardy. A young nurse grabbed a torch and held it for the remainder of the operation. That nurse was smiling. He counted his task as a privilege – the privilege of being a part of something greater, something bigger than himself. His wasn't a huge job – it was just holding a torch. But the small act became great as it served a greater goal – enabling the safe delivery of a child.

The higher the goal, the more likely are the things that serve that goal to become a privilege.

Key 1: A glorious goal

The first key to Helen's profound sense of privilege is that she was captivated by a glorious goal. She wanted to show Christ that she loved Him and to show the world that Jesus was worthy of that love. No matter what happened in her life, Helen wanted to act in a manner worthy of the Gospel of Christ.

That goal was similar to Paul's yearning for the Philippians. In 1:27 he pleads with them, 'Whatever happens, conduct yourselves in a manner worthy of the gospel of Christ.' Paul wanted the Philippians to demonstrate the value of Christ, to show that Christ is worthy of love and trust.

Helen yearned to show that Christ is worthy:

- to people who had never heard the Gospel
- to the people of the Congo
- to her global audiences

That's a glorious goal.

In WEC we have a wonderful statement, very similar to Helen's goal. Surprisingly, it is hidden in our finance policy. But it is very powerful and I love the way it is stated: 'Christ is worthy of our absolute trust.' That's always true. Even if I doubt and maybe don't absolutely trust Him at some moments, He is always *worthy* of our absolute trust.

Helen had such a goal, a glorious goal, to let the world know that Christ is worthy of our absolute trust. She did not succumb to lesser goals like career success or financial security. Her goal was not her needs, her reputation, herself. She was captivated by this higher goal. Therefore everything that contributed to that goal, even costly and sacrificial things, were swallowed up in privilege.

She was like David Livingston, another famous British missionary doctor to Africa. He was asked near the end of his life how he could have made such sacrifices. He is said to have replied, 'I never made a single sacrifice. How could I call it sacrifice, when other men, serving lesser kings, call it privilege?'

Key 2: A gracious gift

The first key to Helen's profound sense of privilege was a glorious goal. The second key was her understanding that she had been given a gracious gift.

If small things, such as the small gift of holding a torch, can be a privilege as it contributes to a glorious goal, how much more can a deep and profound act be a privilege if it contributes to the greater goal? Perhaps that is the deepest of privileges –

the gift of doing something that deeply and profoundly contributes to the goal of showing that Christ is worthy of our absolute trust.

At times, some of us are given the privilege, the gift, of something that deeply shows that Christ is worthy. Helen was given such a 'gift'. This is what Paul is talking about in Philippians.

He starts with this yearning for the Philippians: 'Whatever happens, conduct yourselves in a manner worthy of the gospel of Christ'. He is challenging them to have a glorious goal – the goal of showing Christ is worthy.

Then, in verse 28, he talks of a 'sign': 'This is a sign to them ....' (We'll see in a moment to what the 'this' refers.) It is a sign to who? To unbelievers. To them, as the verse continues, 'that they will be destroyed, but that you will be saved'. Wow, that's a powerful sign. It is a darkness-penetrating sign.

We who work amongst the unreached peoples of the world, people deceived by various religions and the enemy, often wonder what it will take to penetrate such blindness. And here it is! Paul is speaking of a powerful sign that penetrates the spiritual darkness of unbelievers.

Paul continues in verse 29 by saying, 'For [or, because] it has been granted to you'. That verb 'granted to you' in the Greek actually means 'given a gracious gift', or privilege. There's the gift. God has been gracious to you followers of Christ, Paul says. He has given you a 'gracious gift'.

And what is that gift? That sign? Paul says it has been granted to you 'not only to believe in him, but also to suffer for him'. That's it. The gracious gift, the powerful and darkness-penetrating sign, the privilege is to believe and to suffer – together. It is not just believing. It is not just suffering. It is believing and suffering together. Being able to believe, to trust, in the midst of suffering.

God gave a gracious gift to Helen Roseveare – the gift of suffering. But she not only had the gift of suffering; she also had the gift of believing and trusting in the midst of suffering. She had both together ... in the same gift.

What is my reaction to this? I think if God offered me the same circumstances of this combined gift, I might just take the first part, the believing part! Maybe I would express this as: 'I don't want to be too greedy.

I'll just take this half of the gift. You can give the other half, the suffering half, to someone else!' Perhaps I'd effectively think: 'I'll believe in the good times, in prosperity, in blessings, and let all of that point to Christ as worthy. Surely one could point to Christ as worthy in the midst of blessings ...?'

But there is a deeper privilege and a more profound gift. God doesn't give it to everyone, at least not in the same measure, yet there is the gift to suffer ... and to believe. That's the gracious gift that was given to Helen. And she counted it as a privilege because it contributed all the more towards her glorious goal.

How was that the case? If you believe in the midst of suffering ... If you trust in suffering... If you've lost things, even significant things, yet retain some joy and trust ... then it must mean that you have something of greater value that remains. It points to that greater treasure. It points to Christ – that Christ is worthy of our absolute trust.

That's a powerful sign. And for Helen, that was a privilege. That 'gracious gift' of suffering and believing contributed to her 'glorious goal' ... and so she counted it as a privilege.

The privilege of suffering and believing

Helen Roseveare counted her life as a privilege – in the deepest sense. She was captivated by the glorious goal. As a result:

- she wanted Jesus to know how much she loved Him
- she wanted Jesus to be uplifted and glorified
- she wanted those peoples who had never heard of Christ to know that Christ is worthy of our absolute trust
- she wanted us, you and me, who knew her and read her books and listened to her speak to know that Christ is worthy

In order to contribute to that glorious goal, she was given a gracious gift – the gift of suffering ... and believing ... together. She did suffer. Her 'branches' were broken off, one by one. Her rough spots were polished. But through it all she also believed, trusting deeply that this was all for good. She understood that God was making her into a polished arrow for His quiver, that through Helen He could display His splendour.

May we too be captivated by such a glorious goal, resisting the world's pressure to be attracted to the lesser goals of self and success as the world defines them. May we be captivated by something bigger than ourselves.

If we have been captivated by such a glorious goal, maybe we too will be given a gift, a gracious gift, like that given to Helen: the gift of suffering and believing. Then when we trust Jesus in our suffering, it will be a powerful sign that Christ is worthy of our absolute trust. And we can count it as a privilege.

About the Author

Dr Helen Roseveare (1925-2016) went to the Congo as a missionary between 1953 and 1973. A pioneer of vital medical work in the rainforests of this region, she had a major impact long after she left. Through many trials, she lived out her life striving to serve her Lord with every day – and encouraging those around her to do the same.

Some of her works include:

Enough
(isbn 978-1-84550-751-0)

Digging Ditches: The Latest Chapter of an Inspirational Life
(isbn 978-1-84550-058-0)

Give Me This Mountain
(isbn 978-1-84550-189-1)

He Gave Us a Valley
(isbn 978-1-84550-190-7)

Living Faith: Willing to be Stirred as a Pot of Paint
(isbn 978-1-84550-295-9)

Living Fellowship: Willing to be the Third side of the Triangle
(isbn 978-1-84550-351-2)

Living Holiness: Willing to be the Legs of a Galloping Horse
(isbn 978-1-84550-352-9)

Living Sacrifice: Willing to be Whittled as an Arrow
(isbn 978-1-84550-294-2)

Christian Focus Publications

Our mission statement –

STAYING FAITHFUL

In dependence upon God we seek to impact the world through literature faithful to His infallible Word, the Bible. Our aim is to ensure that the Lord Jesus Christ is presented as the only hope to obtain forgiveness of sin, live a useful life and look forward to heaven with Him.

Our books are published in four imprints:

CHRISTIAN
FOCUS

Popular works including biographies, commentaries, basic doctrine and Christian living.

CHRISTIAN
HERITAGE

Books representing some of the best material from the rich heritage of the church.

MENTOR

Books written at a level suitable for Bible College and seminary students, pastors, and other serious readers. The imprint includes commentaries, doctrinal studies, examination of current issues and church history.

CF4•K

Children's books for quality Bible teaching and for all age groups: Sunday school curriculum, puzzle and activity books; personal and family devotional titles, biographies and inspirational stories – because you are never too young to know Jesus!

Christian Focus Publications Ltd,
Geanies House, Fearn, Ross-shire,
IV20 1TW, Scotland, United Kingdom.
www.christianfocus.com

10Publishing
a division of 10ofthose.com

10Publishing is the publishing house of 10ofThose. It is committed to producing quality Christian resources that are Biblical and accessible.

www.10ofthose.com is our online retail arm selling 1000's of quality books at discounted prices. We also service many church bookstalls around the UK and can help your church to set up a bookstall. Single and bulk purchases welcome.

For more information contact: sales@10ofthose.com or check out the website: www.10ofthose.com